~SOUNDINGS~

Exploring the Depths of God and the Universe

D1520432

Frank L. Jordan III

To Nicki and Cary,
A Joyous Christmas and a.
Happy New Year to you and yours!
Your loving Nephew,
Frank L. Jordan III

PRESS 333

Norfolk, Virginia

Dec 17, 2011

PRESS 333

PO Box 9785

Norfolk, VA 23505

www.press333.com

Cover image: This composite picture of the Helix Nebula,
often called the Eye of God, was created by the National
Aeronautical and Space Administration (NASA) and the
European Space Agency (ESA).

ISBN-13: 978-0-6155-5462-4

ISBN-10: 0-6155-5462-8

For my mother and father—of the Silent Generation,
my wife—of the Baby Boom Generation,
my daughter—of Generation X,
my son and stepdaughter—of Generation Y,
and my granddaughter—of Generation Z,
and really ...

For all of their generations

CONTENTS

Introduction

God is real. I know that God is real because I've personally experienced the love, presence, and power of God at key points in my life. Usually these have been times of extreme crisis, but God's love has flowed during good times also. The elation I felt when my two children were born was from God, although I didn't fully realize it at the time. The enveloping love that grew over a four-day religious retreat took me by surprise.

I've also experienced God's transforming power during many of the realizations I had that make up the contents of this book. I consider most of these "good time" experiences. But some of the realizations came only after I had a profound conversion experience, a conversion that occurred during one of the worst crises of my life. At one point in our marriage, my previous wife and I were on the brink of a serious separation when I realized that I would never be the father that I had always wanted to be for our children—our daughter, then eight, and son, seven—and that that would hurt them. All of a sudden this incredible love swept over me, filling my heart with joy, and I knew it was from God. I knew it was God's love because there was a presence and a power to it. This love knew me intimately, was closer to me than my very breath.

Even though my previous wife and I did still separate for a few months, this life-changing event was key to us being able to reunite at that time. We would remain together for ten more years, years that I'm certain helped shape our children into the wonderful young people that they now are. I am proud to have been their full-time, live-in dad during that time.

It was from this conversion experience that I learned that God is Pure Love, that he loves us passionately, and that there are times when this love breaks through in a profound way. I can't say for certain, but it's possible that some of the realizations I had before my conversion—many of which are found in this book—could have contributed to my being able to receive that experience when I did. God only knows where I would be, and how my children's lives would have been impacted, if I hadn't received it.

The views put forth here—my soundings—took many years to develop. They have enabled me to reconcile aspects of my faith with much that modern science has to teach us. They have offered me comfort and peace during the deaths of all four of my grandparents in the same year, the loss of a close aunt to colon cancer, the tragic death of my younger brother in a car crash, and the loss of a beloved stepmother to Alzheimer's. They helped me make sense of the world when my defenses came crashing down in the midst of an emotional breakdown— an episode that has even worked its way into the pages of this book, and will resonate in me for the remainder of my days.

I offer these soundings as a possible comfort and support to others. I don't believe these poetic essays will in themselves *save* anybody. Only the Spirit of God can do that. But I do believe that they offer unique, contemporary explanations for many of the dynamics between God and the natural universe—

explanations that could help tear down some of the walls between us and Pure Love. In the process, I've tried to articulate with some clarity a worldview that is often otherworldly. I hope I've succeeded.

God knows I've tried.

PART I

The Essentials

Manifestation

I can't escape these thoughts when gazing out on Creation,
  on how maybe *Creation* is a somewhat misleading word,
    implying that nature is the result of an activity
    of the Creator alone,
      when it's obviously more complicated than that.
So with an open heart and mind, I send out my questions,
  my yearnings for answers,
    like soundings,
    and receive these impressions,
      like echoes from the depths of time.

I believe that God, who is Pure Love,
  first created space, and then tremendous energies.
They moved—and time began.
Eventually, as the universe cooled and expanded,
  these energies condensed into matter,
    becoming the basic chemical elements
    of hydrogen and helium.
Gravity worked on these elements, forming the stars.
Within the cores of these stars,
  thermonuclear fusion bound the nuclei
    of hydrogen and helium into heavier elements,

which were eventually scattered
    throughout the universe.

God, who is Ultimate Reality and Truth,
    would not bring into existence
        anything less than real or true, it would seem.
With this in mind, could the newly created universe—
    the early space-time continuum—
        have been anything other than it was?
Could the primordial light and elements,
    with their forces of electromagnetism and gravity,
        have been anything other than they were?
God, who is Ultimate Truth, manifests that which is true,
    making the universe, in the beginning,
        a basic *manifestation* of God.
Is it possible that the universe had to be what it was,
    that it was essential that it be what it was?
The answer to this question is a resounding *Yes!*

The universe has changed since the beginning.
And theories have been devised to explain these changes—
    some supported by evidence, some not.
Let's say that our planet did condense, cool, solidify,
    that our oceans and atmosphere
        did gradually form over time.
Were these direct acts of God, who is Pure Love?
Or is it possible they were the essential developments
    of a combination of elements being worked upon
        by gravity, over time—
            natural elements that must be what they are,
                gravity and time being what they must be,

and all of these being governed by laws
  that must be what they are,
    only that which is true
      being manifested by God, who is the Truth,
      only that which is real deriving from God,
      who is the Ultimate Reality?

To embrace these possibilities
  is to embark on the philosophical journey
    of *derivism.*

Collaboration

Our planet stabilized, was ready for life.
But how did the creation of life occur?
Was it an act of the Creator alone,
    with no input from matter,
        some now more complex?
There is a yearning within that which is manifested
    by Pure Love,
        a yearning to expand,
            to unite in order to become something more.
Like crystallizing minerals, the elements themselves
    yearned to develop.
This is part of the truth of their reality,
    a reality that is derived from God.

As the elements yearned,
    so God met them in their yearning—
        for Pure Love would fulfill every authentic need.
The elements—some now forming more complex molecules—
    yearned to develop, to expand,
        to go where they didn't know where to go—
        to change, to be transformed,
            to reach out with yearning, in freedom.

The need is deep enough, the desire complete.
God meets complex matter, in freedom,
   imbues it with power—
      and life is born on earth.
For God is the Source of life.

Living cells, having more complex needs—
   to eat, to grow,
      to reproduce, to thrive.
A new phase of Creation is risen from the ashes of the old,
   feeds upon the ashes of the old.

This Creation is more than an act of the Creator alone.
It is more like a *collaboration*.
That which is manifested by God,
   that which is real and true,
      yearning for that which only God can supply,
      yearning freely, completely,
         and being touched by Love—
         changed, transformed, brought to life.

And this is only the beginning.

Processes

Just as the natural elements,
    comprising a manifestation of God,
        are indispensably what they are,
            so too are many of the phenomena, laws,
                and processes surrounding the elements.
Once life came into existence
    many of these processes began.

One of the first to begin was the process of respiration,
    which at present is the absorption of oxygen
        and the releasing of carbon dioxide by an organism.
On the cellular level, this oxygen is burned
    with various foods to give living cells energy.

Another such process—found in plants, most algae,
    and many forms of bacteria—is photosynthesis,
        which is when these species use energy from sunlight
        to convert carbon dioxide and water into their own food.
Photosynthesis is a process that also causes oxygen
    to be released from these organisms,
        a supply of oxygen that is absolutely necessary
        for them—as well as humans and lower animals—

to engage in the life-sustaining process of respiration.

Also essential for lower animals and humans to thrive
   is the food stored in many plants and algae,
      for it is with these plants and algae that the food
      lower animals and humans use originates.
It is the consumption of organic nutrients
   such as proteins, carbohydrates, fats, and vitamins,
      and of inorganic nutrients such as water and minerals,
      that makes up a third process
         surrounding the existence of life—
         a process that must be what it is.

It is through the digestion of such organic nutrients as food
   that a type of fuel—first stored in plants and algae,
      and then transferred through the food chain—
      is supplied to the cells of a lower animal or human.
This fuel is oxidized, slowly burned,
   releasing energy that the body uses
      to perform every kind of motion,
      internally as well as externally—
         even the motions of thoughts,
         the movements of feelings.

Did God, did Pure Love and Wisdom
   (which is pure knowledge imbued with love)
      freely create these life processes out of the blue?
The answer is—*not exactly.*
It's possible that respiration, photosynthesis,
   the consumption of all nutrients in general,
      and the digestion of organic nutrients in particular,

are now, as they were in their beginnings,
indispensable phenomena deriving
from realities that life is built upon,
such as light, the elements, gravity, time,
and the laws that govern them—
realities that have to be what they are.

From the moment life came into being,
respiration had to take place,
nutrients had to be consumed and digested,
and photosynthesis had to occur—
once plants, algae, and bacteria came into existence.
The reality of life existing automatically gave birth
to the realities of the processes
that provide life with energy,
that maintain life and enable it to grow.
And all realities are found in God.

This outlook can be applied to a myriad of life processes.
The reality of sleep is an essential product
of a living organism.
Where there is life, there is rest
in the form of the sleep-state.
However, all sleep is not exactly the same.
The sleep of a butterfly is different from human dreaming,
but the difference is more one of *degree* than *kind*.
The sleep of humans must replenish
the complex human organism—
the simpler butterfly sleep, butterflies.
However, all sleeping—like eating or drinking or breathing—
has to be what it is.

And then there's reproduction.
The differences in consumption and sleeping
   cannot compare to the differences in reproduction.
How can the splitting of an amoeba
   be compared to the procreation of a human—
      beginning with sex between a man and woman,
      and culminating with birth?
Both are acts of reproduction, but both are so different.
The sameness results from the fact
   that both are living organisms.
The differences have to do with the fact
   that both organisms are separated by evolution.
But generally speaking, reproduction must be what it is—
   although some unique characteristics have developed
      because of the needs of particular life forms.

Recapping on some ideas before moving on …

The origin of the universe
   was a basic manifestation of God,
      who is Pure Love.
As a result, early natural phenomena—
   like light, the chemical elements, time,
      and the laws that govern them—
      were what they had to be,
         realities deriving from God,
         who is the Ultimate Reality.
This philosophical outlook is called derivism.

It is the nature of the elements to develop,

to become more complex.
This yearning to become more is met by God,
and life is born—through collaboration.

With the existence of life comes life processes
that are as indispensably what they are
as the realities of light, the natural elements,
electromagnetism, gravity,
and the laws under which they operate.
Some of these life processes are respiration, photosynthesis,
the consumption and digestion of nutrients, sleep,
and reproduction.

With this in mind,
let's move on to the development of all life
as we know it
within the natural universe.

Evolution

In order for life to develop as a whole,
   forming an ecology within an environment
      that is often hostile to it,
      a plan must be followed.
Who knows this better than God?

Our world's biology must be an intricate fabric
   of mutually supportive species—
      some feeding, some being fed upon,
      some cooperating, some competing,
         some living, some dying,
         some sacrificing, some partaking of the sacrifice.
To put it bluntly, the indispensable ecology
   of our world having to be what it is
      derives from the indispensable nature
      of the elements, of life, and of life's processes
         having to be what they are.
A plan must be followed.

God is the author of the forms of life.
The vast majority of plants must have roots,
   a stem or trunk, branches, leaves.

God patterns most higher life forms to have sense organs,
   a head containing a brain, a body—
      with body parts to transport the species,
        to experience sexual pleasure and reproduce,
          or to manipulate the species' environment.
But the individual species are given creative freedom
   as they evolve from simple to more complex organisms.

Each species supplies the need to adapt to its environment,
   the yearning to survive, to reproduce,
      to protect itself, to find shelter, to progress,
      to express itself, to love.
God supplies the power to each species, to all species,
   to achieve these goals.
But God tempers the achievements
   of each species (except one)
      in consideration for the world's ecology as a whole.
Notice how it all works so well together—
   except for diseases, accidents, hostile weather,
      natural disasters, and evil.
But these are topics in themselves, for another time.

Here is an explanation of the development of a species
   in light of this philosophy.

A small horse-like creature needs to survive.
   Its need is strong.
It has been food for fearsome felines once too often.
God recognizes this need,
   knows the creature's every fiber,
      knows the environment it thrives in

like the back of an omnipresent hand.

God knows what would make things more difficult
for the creature's predators.
So God, with fathomless love and knowledge,
empowers the creature with a defense—
one written on its very hide.
And, over time, the zebra has its stripes.

In a pack, the stripes twist and merge,
making the individual zebra harder to spot,
giving the species the edge that it needs,
not to mention a bit of self-expression—
a collaborative effort, these stripes.

This approach to evolution can be applied to
thousands of life forms—plant and animal.
Have fun.
I suspect God does …
especially with the primates.

Humanity

There is within this unfolding manifestation of God,
    the natural universe,
        a strain of life which is very close to God's essence.
From the moment life was born on Earth,
    the potential for this strain existed and began to develop,
        soon coursing its way through natural history.
Being close to the very Spirit of Pure Love,
    this life sought the highest expression—
        seeking ever to improve, to be improved,
        to experience God's love and approval.

Where other life forms evolved to the summit
    of becoming the species currently found today,
        and were content before God,
        this life form was never fully content—
            never fully satisfied or at rest
            until it rested in the precious power
                and love and knowledge of God.
This strain of life moved through the primates,
    alongside the ancestors of the great apes,
        but did not stop there.
Turning to God for its survival,

development, and expression,
  with all the power of its unique yearning,
  this species was empowered by God
    to best reflect Pure Love in the universe—
    reflect God's intelligence, emotions, sexuality,
      protectiveness, creativity, language,
      memory, inventiveness, productivity,
        wisdom, humor, mercy ...

This life blossomed into humanity, by God's touch,
  in collaboration with its unique yearning—
    became men and women, of many colors.
And it would seem, they tasted of their destiny.
It would also seem, God saw them as very good.

With the advent of human consciousness in the world,
  there came into existence a great paradox.
The early humans were the first to conceive of God as holy,
  powerful, loving, and all-knowing.
They often experienced God's presence and love directly.
But they also suffered greatly.
  They felt pain, hunger, fear.
  They knew disease.
  They had accidents.
Sometimes the environment turned against them.
They encountered evil,
  within themselves and among each other.

If God is good,
  if God loved them and wanted to help them, heal them,
    had the power to save them from suffering,

why were they allowed to suffer?

This is the great paradox—
    imperfect creatures in an imperfect world,
      suffering in the presence of an all-knowing,
      all-loving, and all-powerful God.

And from the earliest of times this paradox
    has caused a multitude of barriers
      to arise within the hearts and minds of humans,
      inner walls between them and God,
        barriers of anger, hurt, shame,
        confusion, and isolation—
          barriers that have followed humanity
          into the present day.

The fact is that simply existing as a human being
    is a barrier within itself.
The phenomenon of a bio-physical organism—
    a species that emerged
      from practical nothingness and unknowingness
      to reach the summit of human consciousness—
        is nothing short of a miracle.
But it is a miracle that God has wrestled with over untold eons,
    an emerging miracle that God wrestles with today.

For the human brain truly consists
    of the basic essential elements
      having evolved over millions of years
      into an intricate flesh-web of sensitive gray matter,
        complex chemical compounds,

and minute electrical discharges.
And when these phenomena are set in motion
and sustained by a human spiritual entity—
yes, a spiritual entity deriving from and very close to
the Ultimate Spiritual Entity which is God—
then the human brain is a human mind,
which is really how any human brain
comes into existence and is formed anyway,
through the activity of a human spiritual entity,
derived from God.

Any separation of a human brain and a human mind
really only takes place when the brain
is no longer living, no longer functioning.
Before this it is a phenomenon that is truly
a blending and merging—a human brain-mind.
It is a phenomenon governed by the same processes
of respiration, digestion, sleep, and reproduction
that has nurtured life from the beginning.
Yes, the human brain-mind is, barring the discovery
of a higher extra-terrestrial species,
the very pinnacle of the natural universe—
this unfolding manifestation of God.

And God *contends* with that manifestation.
God wrestles with it.
For God who is Pure Love, personified,
God who is pure knowledge imbued with love,
which is Wisdom,
God who is equally feminine and masculine,
perfectly, as is reflected in the universe,

God who is all-seeing, all-knowing,
all-loving, and all-powerful
contends with the power of his,
of her manifestation—
a manifestation that derives its very power
and reality from God.

To view this truth as a limitation of our wonderful God
is a mistaken perception.
The reality of the power of the sacred Spirit of God
exerted in its fullness upon the natural world,
resulting in the development of life
through planetary history,
and climaxing with the advent of humanity—
this reality doesn't limit or lower God,
rather it raises the universe
to its true significance and worth.

It raises the preciousness of life
as it is reflected in God's eyes.
It raises God's people, every human being,
to a deeper understanding of their roles
as collaborators in God's plan,
as laborers of God's love—
and sometimes, as those in need of special care.

The misconceptions surrounding God's activity
in relation to the universe begin when we confuse
what God's power actually is
with what we imagine it to be.
Just because we can imagine God's power

being exerted on physical objects
like an actual hand would be exerted,
doesn't mean that God actually works that way.

It seems very possible that the way God works—
maybe the way God must work
in accordance with reality—
is through the hearts and minds
and limbs of living things,
that this is the essential avenue
through which miracles occur,
especially within the human arena.

This belief that God struggles with the natural universe
in bringing about positive change is called *contention,*
and is a vital aspect of derivism.

The awareness of God contending with the universe in general,
and with the hearts and minds of humans in particular,
can help us to understand
why circumstances occur that cause us to suffer—
why we experience suffering in the first place.

It can help us to understand
why we experience God the way we do,
and why we often feel or think
we aren't in touch with him,
aren't experiencing her,
much at all.

Presence and Absence

What does it mean to know God as Pure Love?
It means knowing that God gives us everything he can.
It means knowing that God loves us unconditionally,
    no matter what we've done or are doing,
        no matter what we've been or are becoming.

God is Pure Love.
Pure Love gives everything possible.
    Pure Love withholds nothing.
Pure Love wants to give us comfort, support,
    nurturance, power, confidence, healing,
        knowledge, wisdom, forgiveness, and more.
God wants to give us all of this,
    and something far more precious than all of this.
God wants to give us his, to give us her very *self*.
And sometimes in our lives we experience this,
    and many times we don't.

Why?

Because God attempts to offer us these precious gifts
    while contending with our natural selves.

Our natural selves—physically, chemically,
emotionally, mentally, and spiritually—
are the highest life forms yet known
within this unfolding manifestation of God,
this emerging collaboration of nature with God.

All that we are that is healthy and good,
all that we've experienced individually,
as families, and as a people
that has been constructive and helped us grow
is proof of God's giving.

All that we are that is unhealthy and evil,
all that we've experienced individually,
as families, and as a people
that has been destructive and hurt us
is proof that God wants to give more.

During every moment, at this moment,
God offers all that he, all that she *is*!

But our natural selves—our bodies, our brains,
our hearts and minds—
are not fully able to receive,
to utilize this offering of God
at this point in time,
at this stage of our development.

Don't get me wrong.
There are ways to gain a greater access to God,
just as there are methods to nurture

the experience of God we have now.
They are well known—prayer, meditation, worship,
    contemplation, creativity, study, research, and discovery.
And there are those rare persons
    who have a special talent for these practices
        that has enabled them to gain a much greater access
        to Pure Love than the rest of us.

There are also those circumstances of life
    that can cut to our very cores,
        the ones that break through our human barriers,
        that strip away our defenses,
            leaving us bare and vulnerable—
            open to God in a way that we usually aren't,
                needing God more deeply than we usually do,
                to experience God in a way
                    that we usually don't,
                    to swim in God, usually for a limited time.

But those persons and these events
    are precious and rare, like jewels.
If we don't encounter them, or run from them when we do,
    then our relationship with God can stagnate,
        or worse yet, regress.

Our experience of God,
    as a race of beings growing closer to him, to her that *is*
        can be compared to the light spectrum.
The way in which the vast majority of us
    are currently aware of God
        is like the portion of the light spectrum

we call visible light.
Different persons perceive different aspects of it.
This segment of *visible light consciousness*
 allows for many different kinds of perceptions,
  and therefore, opinions.
It represents an area of great spiritual subtlety,
 where God can be so transparent
  that we sometimes question
  the existence of the Spirit at all.

It is a consciousness that allows
 for the atheist and the agnostic,
  who offer up arguments that sometimes
  create reasons to doubt.
It is an area that relies heavily on ancient testimony,
 when our race was younger,
  when the line between myth and daily reality
  was not so clearly drawn—
   when signs and wonders rose up
   to meet our ancestors on dusty roads.

This current state of awareness often trusts
 in the revelations and promises of God
  given to these ancestors,
  while such gems are much scarcer today.
Still, our collective modern spirituality,
 our *visible light consciousness*,
  hopes and prays for a clearer understanding,
  a heightened awareness.

Sometimes, some people are granted it—or born with it.

PRESENCE AND ABSENCE

Sometimes, an inner mechanism, like some new transistor,
    is activated somehow within a person,
        and an unseen frequency is tapped into.
When this is communicated to the rest of us,
    our awareness of this light spectrum is broadened,
        enhanced, amplified,
        and we all grow from the experience.
But our growth is tempered by our natural limitations
    at this stage of the game.

So collectively, as a people,
    we are all in the same developmental boat, spiritually.
Many mull about in the hull, while a few work the deck,
    and a handful mount the masts,
        but we are all in it together.

But why the sometimes terrifying seas?
Why the vulnerabilities of these bodily vessels?
    And why the mutiny in our hearts?
And where is our lifeguarding Captain,
    our guiding Light?

It has been theorized that God withholds
    healing and sustenance and companionship
        until we turn to him of our own free will,
        until we change our ways.

I don't believe it.

The God I know doesn't willingly permit people to suffer,
    allow children to die,

while we decide whether or not
we're going to surrender our hearts to him.
For one thing, there are people every day
who submit to God's will,
make a good, hard, honest attempt,
and still feel distant from God—
sometimes for most or all of their lives.

No, God does not place conditions on his, on her love and care,
but loves us unconditionally, loves all life unconditionally.
Pure Love offers us everything we need,
wants so much to give it.
But God contends with the intrinsic power of the universe,
of this unfolding manifestation of God.

God, who is the Ultimate Reality,
works in collaboration with the realities
brought into existence—to further their development.
However, some realities are more pliable
or cooperative than others.

Our reception of God's presence and power is a process,
like the process of all of Creation.
The development of our universe and ourselves
is like a baby's formation and birth.
It germinates, it grows.
It undergoes interior processes, it is ready.
It is born.

It knows life,
with all of life's pleasures and pains.

Sensation

Life begets sensation.
As a life form evolves, develops,
   the complexity of the sensations it experiences develops.
To live is to feel, to see, to hear,
   to taste and smell,
      to experience emotions, thoughts—
      an inner flow of ebbs and tides.

All life forms experience these things to some degree.
Whether it be a flower turning toward the sun,
   or a woman turning toward her lover,
      sensation is present, for sensation is life itself.
So to be a more highly developed life form
   means to experience life's sensations more deeply, clearly.

Look at the canine, with its superior sense of smell,
   being able to detect the scent of a subject,
      follow the trail left,
      long after that subject has passed through the air.

Look at the feline, with its superior eyesight,
   being able to detect shapes and track them

in the virtual absence of light.

Look at us human beings,
   who, in the throes of sexual pleasure,
     can be shaken from head to toe—
     who, in the clutches of emotional upheaval
      can be driven to our very knees.

Yes, to live is to experience sensation,
   and for there to be sensation,
     there must be the possibilities of pleasure and pain.
For the same living tissues that make sensations possible
   are the same living tissues that register pleasure
     if exposed to nurturance,
     and pain if exposed to violence.

Pleasure and pain are the flip-sides of the same coin,
   that coin being sensation.

To see is a pleasure, to lose one's sight is painful.
To hear is a joy, to lose one's hearing, an ache.
To touch is stimulating, to lose one's sense of touch,
   an emptiness.
To live without violence
   is to experience healthy and joyful sensations.
To live with violence
   is to have joyful sensations interrupted,
     to have them replaced with pain, sometimes agony.

Yes, it is essential for there to be the possibility of pain
   for there to be the reality of sensation.

SENSATION

This is a principle as basic as the existence of life itself.

The reality of pain is not conjured up by God
    as some sort of learning experience for us,
        for all living things.
The reality of pain is intertwined within the very fabric
    of this evolving universe.
It is an actual aspect of the unfolding manifestation of God,
    of this continuing collaboration of nature with God.

So is the reality of pleasure,
    although an understanding of pleasure is less intriguing.
We simply enjoy it, pursue it, long for it—
    not really caring so much why.
But pain is another story.
It can consume us, overwhelm us.
It has the potential to drive us deep within ourselves,
    crying out, reaching out with a yearning
        and longing for release,
            for something, *someone*, to deliver us.

Yes, it seems that the deepest growth of a living being
    usually occurs during life's more painful episodes.
And for the most part, the appreciation of the joys of life
    are experienced at the level of inner growth
        that one has already achieved.

For instance, one who has lost his or her spouse
    will often emerge from the grieving process
        a stronger, more sympathetic person.
Whereas someone who has won a lottery

might experience great elation,
    but their level of personal growth
    remains basically the same.
This even holds true for the joy
    resulting from an accomplishment.
It's not the joy that causes the actual growth,
    but the discipline and sacrifice involved,
      the struggle endured.

However, although suffering in life carries with it
    the possibility of strengthening character,
      it by no means guarantees the certainty
      of such growth.
For the outcome of a person's encounter with pain
    is determined by how constructively or destructively
      that person deals with it,
      and often, how well that person shares
        their suffering, their loss, with God.
For really all suffering, all pain,
    involves the loss of something.
Even a minor injury means losing a certain degree
    of comfort or mobility, or both.
Show me a painful experience that does not involve a loss,
    and I'll show you a loss well hidden.

For even the pain of a desire unfulfilled,
    of something not yet attained, involves a kind of loss.
Because there was a previous time
    when that desire didn't exist or was sleeping,
      when one was content with a lack,
      was innocent of a want or need.

SENSATION

It was a time, now lost, gone with lost innocence—
    like when there is the ache for sexual union
        only after one's sexuality awakens,
        only after that innocence is lost.
But how well we deal with such longing,
    or really how well we deal with any pain or loss,
        depends on how constructive or destructive
        our approach is, our attitude is.
And how constructive or destructive we are towards others
    concerning our own suffering
        is determined by how thoroughly and genuinely
        we share our painful experiences with God.

Sharing our pain with God,
    yes, sharing anything with God for that matter,
        is not always easy, far from it.
For many circumstances of our existence, many realities,
    can become obstacles to our sharing with God,
        to our experience of Pure Love.
I believe that certain circumstances of life become obstacles
    because we have a limited understanding
        of the relationship between God,
        these circumstances, and ourselves.
And while these obstacles are numerous for adults,
    they can be even more numerous for children,
        because children are particularly vulnerable
        to the debilitating effects of life's harsher realities.

Children need to be loved, protected,
    nurtured and cared for—
        at least until they can care for themselves,

and often longer.
If they don't receive adequate care,
    then a painful experience can become traumatic,
        can scar a child's psyche,
        can become an obstacle between that child
            and his or her joyful, loving feelings—
            can alienate that child from himself or herself,
                others, and God.

And where there is trauma and alienation,
    there is paralysis and fear.
Their actual hearts—those well-springs of joy
    and deep, abiding love,
        beating with the promises of childhood—
        can become scarred and broken,
            slowly dwindling into numb emptiness.
And where there are broken hearts,
    sensation is lost, life goes into hiding,
        for so much of life is sensation.

So while we as adults strive for understanding,
    while we pursue our happiness,
        and confront our private demons,
        the needs of children, all children,
            must ever be before our eyes.
For they are entitled to a healthy, happy start,
    a solid footing amidst the shifting sands of life,
        so that whatever circumstance meets them,
            it will find them with sound minds and loving hearts—
            hearts full of rich sensations.

PART II

The Effects

Chance

How do we arrive at a deeper understanding
  of the circumstances of life,
    circumstances that can bring us pain, joy,
    and the wide range of experiences in between?

To begin to have a deeper understanding of life's events,
  a very basic property of life should be examined.
For of all of the elements
  that affect our experience of reality,
    few do so more profoundly
    than the element of chance.
But what is chance?
And how does it fit into the scheme of things?

Chance is a reality of existence
  which is especially removed
    from the activity and influence of God,
    and from those life forms
      which collaborate with God
      in their own development.
But chance can be a substantial occurrence,
  depending on its effect.

The possibility of chance is built
   into the very fabric of this universe.
From the moment there were two or more energies,
    two or more elements, two or more gravitational fields,
     two or more planets, two or more environments,
     two or more life forms, or two or more communities,
      there existed the possibility
       that any one or more of these things
        would affect any other
        one or more of these things
         in a random way, or in random ways.

God did not create chance.
Chance is an essential reality within a universe
   in which energies and matter move,
    in which environments and life forms interact,
    in which people and systems connect.

An occurrence is more purely chance
   when the motivating factors behind it
    are less purposeful, less meaningful.
And since God is the author of purpose and meaning,
   the more God's presence and power
    permeate a scenario,
    the less things will be left to chance.

For instance, when the universe was young—
   before life, before birth—
    manifested reality was much more chaotic,
    much more prone to randomness.

CHANCE

But the more influence Pure Love exercised
in the natural world—
the more God molded reality
to better reflect the divine plan—
the more mere chance was abated.

The evolution of life on this planet
has clearly been a slow process of order and diversity
arising out of chaos and randomness.
Yes, there have occurred those cataclysmic events,
like when that stray asteroid struck Earth
some sixty-five million years ago,
filling the prehistoric sky with dust,
and probably choking out the dinosaurs.

But those events are few and far between,
and not what I would call an act of God.
Pure Love doesn't go around guiding asteroids or planets.
It seems that God's methods
of influencing the environment
begin in the hearts and minds of living things,
transforming their yearnings into shapes,
their yearnings creating some
trial and error along the way—
trial and error sometimes
resulting in extinction.

An asteroid the size of Manhattan
is not readily transformed from within,
and is more prone to chance from without.
It's like blindly shooting a load of buckshot

into the sky at noon every day.
Sooner or later you're going to hit something,
   but more often you won't.
The asteroid that most likely wiped out the dinosaurs
   at the end of the Cretoceous period
      could have just as easily missed this planet,
      and we could be arguing with our kids
         about whether they should be getting
         their scales pierced or not!
Not that I really believe that the evolution of humanity
   could have been so deeply affected
   by the omission of one freak event.
But it is possible that if that catastrophe had not occurred,
   we might not be enjoying our present-day status
   at the top of the food chain.

My point is that there has been an element of chance
   running through our universe from the beginning.
But as the universe evolves,
   as this manifestation of God unfolds—
      the collaboration of nature with God emerges—
      the influences of random chance,
         for better or worse, are diminished—
         and it's almost always for the better.

But it helps to put these influences in their place,
   seeing them for what they are—
   events devoid of purpose and meaning,
      sometimes occurring in a world
      full of purpose and meaning,
         among people seeking only to be happy,

CHANCE

only to know their God more deeply,
and coming up against those rare,
but earth-shattering events
that can cut them to their very cores.

It helps to put things in their place,
for the more they are in their place,
the less chance there is
they can become an obstacle
between us and the One
who holds us so dear.

Time

Time is another reality of life
    that has no life of its own, no mind of its own,
      but has such a profound effect
      on the lives and minds of so many.
Depending on these minds and perceptions,
    time can either be viewed as a friend or enemy,
      when in fact it is neither.
Time simply is.
And of all the realities that simply are,
    time holds a special place in God's heart.

For time is the measurement of the interplay
    between all of the realities in the universe.
Wherever the motions of a reality or realities
    are in relation to the motions
      of another reality or other realities,
      there time can be measured.
Where there is no motion, there is no time.
And within this realm all is in motion,
    including that which is touched most
      by the love of God.

Yes, time does not exist in the universe
    for things that are not in motion,
        for things that are not in relation to one another.
This is why time does not exist in the past,
    for the past is but a memory.
It is true that much can be learned from the past,
    that past memory can enable species
        to build skills and grow.
But this truth does not affect
    the absence of time surrounding the past.
Playing back a message recorded in the past
    does not make the past reoccur.
It enables that message from the past
    to have another and sometimes new effect
        on the present.
And in this realm, it is the present moment,
    and the present moment alone,
        that is permeated with the reality of time.

That's why it is so special to God,
    and why it should be sacred to us.
For it is *now*, and only *now*,
    that the relationship between the Spirit of God
        and the manifestation of God occurs.
All else is memory and vision—
    both wonderful things in their place,
        but both things that can obstruct our view
        of God and nature when held too high.

For there can be elements of memory and vision
    that hinder our experiences of the present moment,

that preoccupy our hearts and minds
with yesterday's ghosts and tomorrow's phantoms.
For the further a memory or vision is
from the very heart of God,
the more possible it is for that memory or vision
to become an obstacle to us living out
the fullest experience of this present moment.
The further a memory or vision is from God's heart,
the less real it is,
and the less real the bearer
of that memory or vision is.

So the key is to nourish the memories,
experience the present happenings,
and discover the visions closest to God's memories,
happenings, and visions.
And this is done *now*—
not in the past, for it is dead,
and not in the future, for it has not yet happened,
not even for God.
That's right, not even for God.

This present moment comes ablaze with sacredness
when it is realized that any future moment
has not yet occurred for any particle,
any life form within the universe.
It's possible that God does not actually *see* the future,
because it has indeed not happened yet.
When this is understood, the immense sacredness
of the present moment—of *now*—becomes so much clearer,
the power of *now* becomes so much more alive.

This is not to say that God cannot predict future events,
   because he does, she will!
But this occurs because God, who sees all that is—
   all the memories, happenings, and visions
      of all life forms everywhere—
      who knows the position, strength, and weakness
         of every atom in the universe,
         can predict the directions that those atoms,
            those energies, those life forms,
            those consciousnesses, and those societies
               will take in future moments.

But it's possible that God (O, heresy of heresies!),
   yes, even God is sometimes surprised.

Understanding God's relationship to the past,
   present, and future can level mountains
      of ignorance about just what responsibility
      God has in relation to life's events.
Understanding God's relationship
   to his emerging manifestation,
      her unfolding collaboration,
      can level even more mountains.
But after all, that's what this book is all about,
   and what it hopes to at least partially accomplish,
      over time.

Environments

In order to better grasp a theatrical production,
   it is necessary to know its setting.
In order to more fully understand our existence on Earth,
   it is a good thing to delve into the roots
      of the environment.
How did this planet come to be?
And why are we here, of all places?
It goes something like this …

When the universe was young,
   planets and moons, comets and asteroids
      were randomly formed within countless galaxies.
Planets spun off of stars, gases condensed over time,
   oceans receded over lands—
      for those planets capable of having oceans.

The point is it was a random process.
No invisible finger guided the planets to where they were,
   processes described by the laws
      of gravity and physics did.
Now, many of these planets found themselves
   in orbits that were conducive to life.

A major component of this conduciveness is temperature.
If a planet or moon sustained temperatures
between the approximate freezing
and boiling points of water,
then the birth and development of life was possible.
Possible, that is, if certain crucial elements
were found there in substantial amounts—
elements like carbon, hydrogen, oxygen,
and magnesium.

The truth that life needs
this relatively narrow temperature window
to originate and thrive,
and that life is made of certain elements
and their chemical compounds,
and consumes some of these
and a few others in the forms
of proteins, carbohydrates, and fats—
these truths are part and parcel
of the reality of life itself,
and are indispensably essential
for the possibility of life as we know it
to exist at all.

This window must be what it is.
And where these conditions for life
are found in the universe,
the yearnings of the elements and their compounds
are met and nurtured by God, the Source of life.

It's like a cavern found deep in a mountain,

where there are small holes all over the surface
of that mountain,
allowing tiny beams of light into the cavern.
Only under these beams of light
will green plants sprout and grow.
So it is with celestial bodies that have acquired,
however randomly, the conditions for life.
But once life has originated
and begun the process of evolution—
through the power and guidance of Pure Love—
then the creative act of empowering
non-living molecules into becoming living ones
no longer occurs.

This is why within our current world
of simple and complex organisms,
nowhere is the transformation of the inorganic
into the organic to be witnessed.
Those elemental yearnings within the material world
have already been fulfilled in our planet's deep past.
Now the desires themselves have become more complex,
and will not revert back to the ancient desire
to simply become living.

Even though life can emerge
on countless planets and moons in our universe
whenever certain conditions for life are met,
this does not mean that life will appear
exactly the same—
or be in the same stage of development—
as life on Earth, at any given time.

If it exists, life elsewhere probably does follow
    the same guidelines of formation as it does here on Earth—
        in the forms of plants and animals,
        of microscopic and non-microscopic life.
And the same processes of respiration, digestion, sleep,
    reproduction, evolution, and ecology probably do apply
    to potential life elsewhere in the universe.
But this does not mean that the histories
    of all planets and moons are the same,
        that the histories of the living beings
        on each planet or moon are the same.

For just as the unique planetary history of our Earth
    has affected life on this planet
        in a particular way over time,
        so have the unique histories
            of other habitable planets and moons
            affected life (assuming there is life) elsewhere
                in particular ways over time.
And the arena in which this process has occurred,
    is occurring, and will occur is the environment
    of a particular place.
But how exactly is *environment* defined
    in the present context?

An environment is the sum total of all the objects,
    organic and/or inorganic—
        whether material, mental, spiritual,
        or any combination of these—
            found within a particular place.
The limits of an environment are defined

by the limits put on the term *place*.
We tend to refer to our ecological system on Earth,
the biosphere, as the environment.
And when considering how it can best
be nurtured and maintained,
we human beings tend to set ourselves apart
from the environment, to visualize it more clearly—
like deliberately leaving the trees
to view the forest.
But in actuality we are not only a significant part
of this planet's environment,
human beings are at the pinnacle
of the significance of Earth's ecology.

One of the reasons for this is because we humans,
as extremely sensitive life forms,
are most deeply affected by the realities
we encounter within our environment.
This is not to say that other life forms on Earth
are not deeply affected by the realities
they encounter within their environment.
They are—some nearly as much as us we are.
But here on Earth, human beings have the capacity
to experience life more deeply,
communicate life more articulately,
understand life more fully,
suffer the accidents and evils of life
more profoundly,
desire sex in life and relish its happening
more completely,
hunger and thirst for,

not only food and drink,
but a more genuine experience of living—
and with more yearning.

And this experience of living is crowned
by our relationship with God,
with all that he, all that she *is*.
For it is the coursing of God's love
within our hearts and minds and bodies
that gives us the ultimate fulfillment
during our existence here and now.
Our yearning, our fulfillment is surpassed only
by God's yearning for us, fulfillment in us.
For God is the true Lover of lovers!
We are but disciples of his love, of her desire.
And when God's love permeates an environment,
that environment is changed, transformed.
Deserts become lush, promised lands.
Cracked river beds are filled to overflowing.

But there are times when these kinds of things
are obviously not happening, aren't there?
There are times when other factors burst into our lives
and affect our environment in hurtful, destructive ways.
Accidents and diseases, catastrophes and crises—
all can fill our lives with pain and confusion,
causing us to demand, "God, where are you now?
How could *you*, my Protector, let this happen?!"

Good questions that deserve good answers.

It's so important to comprehend where God stands
in relationship to the realities that affect
our environment in hurtful ways,
for it's only through such a comprehension
that we can become truly free
to fully know and love our kind and loving God.

That's why it's so important to understand that God
does not directly cause pain to occur to any person—
unless it's the emotional pain that someone experiences
when that person has unjustly caused
or is unjustly causing harm to themselves or others,
has lost or is losing the valued company of another,
has lost or is losing the possession or use
of a thing contributing to their own well-being,
has lost or is losing the care or service
of another who has been contributing
to that person's well-being.

This means that the vast majority of hurtful events
that we encounter in this world
are not caused to happen by God,
who is Pure Love,
but much of the emotional suffering
in connection with such events is.
For you see, the pain that God does cause to happen
is more accurately associated with realizations
and feelings of remorse and grief—
for remorse is evidence of the loss of innocence,
and grief is evidence of the loss
of that which is truly loved,

which is the loss of love itself.
The qualities of innocence and love in this world
are particularly valued by our righteous, loving God,
and when we experience their loss
we can and often do experience pain
that is directly willed by Pure Love.
For the pains of remorse and grief
can be like hooks dug deep in our tender hearts,
attached to the lifelines of God's care,
pulling us closer and closer to our Source
of mercy and comfort.

This especially includes the grief we can experience
as we leave behind outmoded characteristics
of ourselves—those lifestyles and habits
that may have served us well in the past,
but are no longer appropriate for us now,
or in the future.
However, apart from all of these kinds of suffering,
it's hard to perceive God directly causing hurtful events—
unless one considers the vanquishing
of an infectious disease through God's healing power
a hurtful event for the disease.
But this falls under the umbrella of a lower life form,
in this case microscopic,
unjustly harming a higher life form,
and thus reaping its just deserts—
that is, when such healing occurs,
which at present seems to be a rare
and sporadic event.

This brings us to the point that,
    although God doesn't cause many
        of life's tragic events to happen,
            it appears that he doesn't intervene very often
                in stopping them from happening either.

A closer look at some of these events,
    and where God stands in relation to them,
        may throw some light on just why.

PART III

The Obstacles

Death

When someone's bodily functions cease
    at the conclusion of a long and productive life,
        when the causes of that dying
        are as natural and painless as possible,
            then it can be said that a person has experienced
            a relatively harmless death.
For death is so natural, so much a part
    of existing in this world,
        that to experience it as a final, quiet passing
        is a blessing—albeit the last blessing
            in a long line of the many blessings
            that can make up an earthly life.

I once heard that in Earth's prehistoric past
    there were organisms that seemed to live forever,
        were virtually immortal—like jellyfish—
        but the price they paid for their immortality
            was that they were unable to progress and evolve.
Then *nature invented death*,
    and the obstacles to evolution were eliminated.
What an intriguing idea, that death was invented
    so that organisms could evolve,

that death was essential for those organisms to evolve.
It kind of puts death in a different light, doesn't it?
Not an altogether positive light,
    but not a negative one either—
        death as a necessity,
            instead of as an unnecessary evil.

But often, quite often, a death is not necessary—
    not by our standards, not by anyone's.

When a disease causes one to die prematurely
    (and a week too soon can be prematurely),
        when an accident ends a young life,
        we are left shocked and confused,
            and depending on our relationship to the departed,
            sometimes totally devastated.

And why not?
We are bound to one another,
    and to our fellow creatures on this planet.
The love and respect we have towards one another—
    and to those animals that we have chosen
        to be a part of our lives—
        that love and respect has emerged
            from the dawn of time to be a dominate impulse
            and emotion in our daily existence.
These are impulses and emotions
    that are the very essence of God,
        and it is God's work and will that love,
        devotion, and protectiveness fill our lives—
            and the life of this planet.

So our devotion to the life and well-being
of others and ourselves,
our dedication to the nurturance
and protection of these lives,
are emotions and realities akin
to the very outpourings of the sacred heart of God.
And yet, sometimes we die prematurely, tragically,
without any or little warning,
victims of forces that seem to mock
the life-embracing purposes of God—
and the purposes of us,
the highest expression yet known within this,
the unfolding manifestation of God.
So where does God stand in relation
to this harsh reality of existence?

I've come to believe that God neither causes nor wills
any human being to die prematurely
from any accident, illness, or animal attack,
from over-exposure to the elements, starvation,
or dehydration—much less from any crime,
recklessness, or suicide.
Apart from the unavoidable death of an assailant
during an act of self-defense by the one being attacked,
the sacrificial death of a firefighter or police officer
in the line of duty,
or of a military person in defense of their community,
country, or country's interests
(or really any true sacrifice of life, for that matter),
the premature death of any human being

is outside of God's will and purposes.

We are all God's children.
Do we want our children to suffer and die early, in vain?
Why would God want *us* to, will us to?
    It wouldn't make sense.
    It doesn't make sense.
But what does make sense is that God
    wants us to live long, happy, healthy lives.
And if our lives must be cut short,
    it should be for a damned good reason,
        like as a sacrifice for another or others.

God is hurt when we die prematurely,
    and particularly heartbroken when we die in vain.
So why does this sometimes happen?

It happens because there are realities in this universe,
    occurrences within this unfolding manifestation
        of God's Ultimate Reality,
        that by the very nature of their existence
            can sometimes hurt us, sometimes kill us.
And God contends with these realities, much like he—
    as the universe undergoes transformation and evolution—
        contends with the realities of elements and energies
        being what they are,
            gravity and electro-magnetism
            being what they are,
                chemical reactions and life processes
                being what they are,
                    the intrinsic natures of plants, lower animals,

and humans, collaborating with him,
being what they are,
the realities of time and chance
being what they are—
all of these things being what they are
because they make up a universe
that derives from the very nature of God.
And to derive from the Someone who is God
is to share in that Someone's boundless
essence and reality.

But the harsh realities that can cause us pain
and premature death do not derive from God
like the universe and its processes do,
although the components of these harsh realities do.
Sometimes a tragic event can be a combination
of chance, timing, and the activity
of an inorganic phenomenon—
like when lightning strikes someone.
Sometimes a tragic reality consists of a hostile virus
or bacteria contaminating the metabolism
of a much more advanced life form than itself,
and damaging that body to the point of death.
Sometimes a deadly event occurs
due to the dementedness of a human mind,
a mind darkened by either hostility, ignorance,
irrational fear and loathing,
dementedness brought on by past traumas,
brain chemistry gone haywire,
or an antisocial make-up—
pure, or better yet, impure evil.

The important thing to remember here is that God,
  our comfort and our strength,
    does not want or cause any of these kinds
    of things to happen.
God loves each and every one of us immeasurably,
  wants only for us to live and grow,
    not suffer symptoms or injuries and die in vain.
So our powerful and loving God is in open opposition
  to those dangerous realities in life that are a threat
    to our safety and well-being.
It is a struggle that at times appears hidden,
  but can become more apparent
    when we know what to look for.

Understanding how God interacts and contends
  with certain life-threatening occurrences
    can help us understand why they occur
    the way that they do,
      and why sometimes they are interrupted
      and cease to occur.
It can help us understand how we as laborers
  of love and enlightenment
    can best join God in the struggle against them,
    how we as a race of beings often have, still do,
      and continue to do so,
        sometimes in amazing, incredible ways—
          ways that can become
          even more amazing and incredible
          in the years ahead.

Natural Disasters

No one understands better than God
  just why natural disasters occur,
    and how they can cause human beings to suffer,
    become injured, or even die.
No one longs more deeply than God
  that we be spared these sufferings,
    injuries, or deaths.

When a devastating hurricane or typhoon makes landfall,
  wreaking untold damage to life and property,
    when a tremendous earthquake
    levels massive buildings and buries people alive,
      when unceasing rains cause flash floods
      that drown people in their tracks,
        and mudslides that engulf whole towns,
      when unrelenting draught
        causes the lushest farmlands
        to become parched and the mightiest of rivers
        to dwindle down to a mere stream,
          leaving people and wildlife to scramble
          for a few precious drops of water,
          when renegade lightening

strikes dried-out trees or brush,
causing furious wildfires
that know no boundaries
and take no prisoners ...
God is watching, knowing,
understanding perfectly
exactly why these phenomena occur.

And why wouldn't he?
The basic ingredients that make up these events
are elements, compounds, and processes
that have been a part of this world,
played a part in its shaping,
since the dawn of time.
They are intimately woven in the very fabric
of an existence consisting of earth, wind,
water, lightning, and fire.
They are the rawest of happenings,
elements, energies, and compounds
whipped into a blind frenzy by powerful forces
that are mostly natural—
rarely, but sometimes, humanly induced.
But even though such occurrences have been a part
of this world for a long time,
even though they might have benefited
this planet's development along the way,
it is not God's will that we humans should suffer,
become injured, or die prematurely
because they occur.
On the contrary, it is God's will that all people be spared
the ill effects of any natural disaster.

Is this surprising?
Is it surprising to expect this of he who is Pure Love,
   of she who is pure knowledge imbued with love,
      which is Wisdom?

We are at the summit of God's creative efforts.
Is it any wonder that God wants us to be safe and secure,
   wants us to be spared the shifting ground,
      whirling wind, or lightning strike?

God loves you!
God wants the environment to nurture you,
   not do you harm.
So if a powerful natural event
   does bring disaster into your life,
      remember,
         God doesn't want you or those you hold dear
            to suffer loss, be hurt, or die as a result of it.
Just because we are wounded by nature's hand
   does not mean that God wills us to be wounded.
Actually, the opposite is true.
It is God's will that we be spared from harm.
In some ways and at some times, this does happen,
   and obviously, in other ways and at other times,
      it does not.

Why?

First, it's important to understand that God
   is doing everything in his, in her power to keep us

from the harm that is brought about
    by natural catastrophes.
There is no lack of effort, love, care, or concern
    on God's part.
But once again, God's will and work is in contention
    with some of the circumstances that occur
        within this realm—
            a realm that we more and more delicately refer to
                as the unfolding manifestation of God,
                the emerging collaboration of nature with God.
(This idea must be becoming more anticipated,
    more recognizable, and more easily applicable.)

Remember, God's influence is being exerted
    in its fullness at this very moment, at every moment.
That is the very essence of Pure Love—
    to offer everything, to withhold nothing.
The awareness of this fact,
    which might initially seem to be
        placing limitations on God,
            in reality reveals the true worth and significance
                of this universe as God's manifestation.
This idea, like many ideas in this book,
    is aimed at gaining a deeper understanding
        of the full implications of what it means
            for something or someone to participate
                in our wonderful God manifesting himself, herself—
                through space and over time.

Different phenomena participate
    in this awesome process in different ways.

NATURAL DISASTERS

Some types of phenomena are by their very natures
    more susceptible to God's direct influence than others.
A general rule would be that the more fully alive,
    the more deeply aware a body is,
        the more capable it is of experiencing the power
        and love and influential guidance of God.

That's why the body of, say, a hurricane or tornado
    is minimally influenced by God's direct power.
That's why these phenomena can cause
    so much devastation to the environment and to our lives,
        when it is God's will
        that we not be harmed or killed by them.
So in order to help bring about
    God's purposes and work in these matters,
        we must seek to cooperate and collaborate
        more fully with our Protector.
This is done in diffcrent ways.

From the ancient days when a person would look
    to the reddened sky at dawn,
        and begin preparations for the coming storm,
        to our modern times when Doppler radar
            can track a hurricane from its origins
            to its dissipation,
                humans have used their increasing powers
                of observation to better protect themselves,
                    their families, and their communities.
With the advent of scientific procedures,
    our ability to monitor and predict natural disasters
        has grown in leaps and bounds.

The intelligence, innovation, and inventiveness
    with which our human race devises ways
        to better observe the environment
        is achieved by collaborating with God and God's will.

For untold centuries we have yearned
    to better observe and understand our environment,
        and God has met our yearnings by giving us
        the power to increase our abilities to do so.
Science has been one of our most loyal helpmates,
    for science seeks only to discover the truth
        about phenomena through objective observation
        and experimentation.
So science is the patient revealer
    of the workings of the universe,
        and it can lead us to the sustaining power
        behind the universe, which is Pure Love.

Another possible way that we humans
    can more fully cooperate with God
        against natural disasters is through intuitive activity.
It is true that authentic psychic phenomena is rare,
    but its rarity does not make it any less real or possible.
The rarity of intuitive activity points to the fact
    that it is an emerging practice,
        that humans are slowly gaining the ability to perceive
        hidden or distant realities intuitively.
And one particular area of intuitive perception
    is the prediction of natural disasters.

When a natural disaster is about to occur, like an earthquake,

God is perfectly aware of the brewing catastrophe.
If a person is substantially intuitively sensitive,
    God can and will communicate this awareness
        to him or her.
As the tensions of this looming disaster build up,
    then it becomes more and more possible to predict
        through intuitive means
        the approximate time it will occur.
Although very rare, this emerging process
    of predicting and preparing for natural disasters
        holds great promise for the future.

But there is a nobler, more exalted method
    of joining efforts with God against natural disasters—
        a way that truly holds the greatest hope for the future.
It is a way that cannot only predict such events,
    but can even alter them in their courses.
It is the deepest form of collaboration with God,
    through the purest means,
        and achieving the most effective results.

In order to discuss this in depth,
    the particular source and medium
        of this *exalted way* must be understood deeply
        in the context of derivism,
            within the arena of human history,
            and in relation to the divine plan and struggle
                for Creation's liberation,
                liberation from forces that would harm
                    the universe's highest known aspect—
                    namely, civilization.

But first things first.

A deepened understanding of the relationship
    between our purposeful God
        and some of this world's more chaotic happenings
        is necessary before we can adequately explore
            this *exalted way*,
            and realize just how full of purpose and meaning
                this way was and *is*—
                and how it comes to us
                    by no accident.

Accidents

Fewer words encompass a wider range
of happenings in this world than that of *accident*.
And although it is possible for an accident
to have an immediate positive result,
the vast majority of accidents result in some form
of suffering and even death.
A closer look at the nature of that broad range
of phenomena known as the *accidental*
will shed some light on just why.

For an accident to occur there is usually an interplay
between three particular realities.
The strength or significance of each of these realities
really determines what kind of accident has occurred,
and even to what degree an event
can be called an accident.
There must be a purposeful subject
affected by an event containing an element of chance,
an event for which someone or something shares
a degree of responsibility—
a degree of responsibility, no matter how small,
for that event occurring.

The more responsibility someone or something shares
    for an event occurring,
        the less that event can be called an accident,
        and, depending on whether the occurrence
            has a negative outcome—
            which the vast majority of them do—
                the more that event can be regarded as a crime.

What's meant by a *purposeful subject* is a being,
    place, or thing brought into existence
        through purposeful means.
The more profoundly evolved the being,
    the more highly developed the place,
        and the more skillfully crafted the thing,
            the more purpose surrounds the subject's very existence.
And the more purpose that permeates
    a being, place, or thing,
        the more God is involved in their existence—
        and the more concern he has for their future.

For God is the weaver of purpose
    and the author of concern.
He strives, every moment, to bring
    more and more loving purpose
        into our world and this universe.
In a world that at its basic level has its share
    of randomness and chaos,
        Pure Love—as a guiding force—works diligently
        in collaboration with nature
            to bring about more and more highly refined
            strains of purpose,

and more harmonious avenues of order.

This is easily witnessed in the great systems of this world,
        systems of culture, politics, entertainment, recreation,
            fine arts, mathematics, religion, philosophy,
            medicine, science, industry, technology—
                and the list goes on and on.
If you can name it, God can claim it,
        claim it as an endeavor of divine concern—
            an endeavor in which he, in which she is willing
            to contend with the harshest realities
                to help bring to its deepest fruition,
                its highest vision.
And one of these harsh realities
        is the realm of the accidental.

God does not cause or will accidents to happen,
        but no one understands better
            why they do happen than God.
The key ingredient behind the occurrence of an accident
        is randomness, is chance—
            something or someone being in the wrong place
            at the wrong time, for little or no reason.
God, who is divinely aware of every situation,
        understands perfectly all of the circumstances
            surrounding any accident.
But the very natures of randomness and chance
        make them realities that are particularly removed
            from God's influence and control.
They are realities that are not guided
        by the purposes of life,

so they are not engaged in the protection of life.
The randomness and chance behind accidents
simply are, simply exist—
for they are the most basic of consequences
in a universe where different things, places,
and beings affect each other.

And along with God not directly causing
any accident to happen,
he also doesn't want loss, injury, or death
to occur to anyone as the result of an accident.
But these things happen—
sometimes to people we love, sometimes to us.

Why doesn't God keep them from happening?

Because the way that God, that Pure Love and Spirit
directly interacts with this world
is not the kind of way that manipulates
physical objects like you or I would.
And this is not a matter of choice on God's part.
It is simply the way things are—
the reality of how God guides and influences
this unfolding manifestation of Ultimate Reality.
But just because it is the nature of things for God
not to directly intervene in a situation
in the same way as a physical being would
does not mean that there aren't ways
that God impacts an event with his power,
influence, care, and concern.
This includes an event that is considered an accident.

Before an accident occurs,
    God is totally aware of the circumstances
        leading up to its potential occurrence.
God knows if an object or machine is about to malfunction,
    because he is aware of every molecule of its structure.
If a human being or lower animal is about to be
    in the wrong place at the wrong time,
        God knows this, also.
And it is God's will that we too have this information.
But for the most part we are not sufficiently attuned
    to the whisperings of the Spirit
        to receive such warnings.

"Why not give a louder or clearer warning?" one might ask.

God gives the clearest, loudest warnings possible.
It's just that the interaction between God pressing through
    into the natural world, into our minds,
        is culminated in the act of intuition—
        a subtle, inner spiritual whispering.
And it is through this medium that warnings
    of future accidents are given and received—
        received, that is, by those few persons
        who are developed or gifted enough
            to intuit and understand them.
When one receives images of a potential accident
    in a dream or vision,
        it should be nurtured and taken seriously,
        for it could be God attempting to warn someone
            of possible harm or of a premature death.

It is God's will that we and those we love,
    lower animal as well as human,
        be spared the devastating effects of accidents,
        and go on to live happy and healthy lives.
This is why the practice of safety
    is such a valued and vital quality within the human race.
We have come to a deeper understanding
    of how certain realities of this world
        can sometimes interact in such a way
        as to bring about a heightened risk
            of possible accidents.
Safety and caution are God-given qualities
    implanted within us to better protect ourselves,
        our families, and our environments.
These two allies have served us well, and continue to do so,
    helping us to avoid much harm and tragedy in our lives.

But obviously accidents can still happen, and when they do,
    when God's cherished ones are hurt or even killed,
        the care and concern that he, that she has for all involved
        can be seen and felt.
Look at how those surviving the accidents of life
    are supported,
        how they are often surrounded
        by compassionate people,
            and nurtured until they are healed.
See how those who do not survive
    are so deeply mourned, honored,
        and remembered over the years.
These life-affirming happenings are inspired by love,

by the very personification of love—our caring God.
They are evidence that even in the darkest times
   of existence God is with us,
      and with those who have gone before us.

But as has already been stated,
   there is an *exalted way* to join with God,
      a way that can warn us of impending disaster,
      deal effectively with it as it is occurring,
         heal the living, and honor the dead
         when the worst occurs.
This way joins the full power of God
   with the potentialities of humanity,
      resulting in an indestructible force
      for good and healing—
         a force that is anything but forceful,
         taming the world into submission
            through unfathomable love and tolerance.

But again, it would be premature to go into detail
   about this *exalted way* before its source is introduced
      in the context of human and divine history.
That can only be done after a clearer understanding
   of some of life's more hostile elements is achieved.
A deeper knowledge of these hostilities of existence
   is necessary before we can fully appreciate
      the overcoming of them.

To embrace a cure,
   we must first understand the disease.

Disease

From the dawn of human consciousness,
   disease has confounded the hearts and minds
      of the people of this world.
Once an ailment was identified
   as a source of suffering and death,
      it was justifiably considered the enemy
      of humankind.
Over scores of centuries, the face and name of that enemy
   has changed as our understanding
      of just what disease is has changed.
What was once attributed to evil spirits
   or to their evil lord, Satan,
      is now understood to be caused by certain bacteria,
      hostile viruses, malnutrition,
         overexposure to occupational hazards,
         environmental pollutants, and mutating cancers—
            or is sometimes rooted in the very recesses
            of one's genetic material.

Although modern knowledge of disease
   has dispensed with many superstitious notions
      once held by our ancestors,

and still held by a few primitive communities today—
    it has not totally unraveled the deepest mysteries
    of many illnesses and why they exist.
For instance, many diseases are caused by living,
    breathing microscopic organisms,
        but it is my understanding that all life
        originates from God.
If God loves us and wants to protect us from harm,
    why does he enable so many hostile organisms
        to live and thrive—organisms that can infect the bodies
        of higher, more developed life forms,
            causing suffering and sometimes death?
What is God's relationship to such microscopic species?

The existence of microscopic organisms—
    both hostile and benign—
        is evidence of a principle that touches on many areas
        concerning the relationship between our God
        and life on this planet.
That principle is that if the need
    to live and thrive is strong enough,
        genuine and authentic enough,
        God will empower any life form to exist.
Because God, the very Source of life,
    would fulfill any and every authentic need to live.
The fact that a life form is unjustifiably hostile
    and destructive to other, higher life forms
        seems to have little bearing on this principle—
        this basic granting of life.
God rains life-giving power on the just and unjust alike.
What purposes a species engages in during their lifetime

is then up to them.
Often, those purposes are openly hostile
to other more highly evolved species.
So when a destructive strain of bacteria or a virus
infects a lower animal or a human,
that particular infected being becomes diseased,
suffers often debilitating symptoms,
and sometimes dies.

This process of contracting an infectious disease
can awaken within us a powerful need of our own—
a need to once again become healthy and whole.
This is a need that our loving God
can and often does fulfill through healing.
For the alleviation of our pain and suffering from infections,
and yes, any other diseases for that matter,
is justifiable cause for the vanquishing
of any hostile microbe, mutating cell,
or genetic defect.
It is God's will that we always succeed
in the battles against diseases that would harm
and sometimes kill us,
and kill the animals (and even the plants)
entrusted to our care.

But obviously we don't always succeed
in our battles against disease.
Sometimes we suffer devastating damage.
Sometimes we die or our loved ones die.

Why?

Because God's will and healing power
   is matched up against the intrinsic powers
      of organisms existing and circumstances occurring
         within a universe that is perpetually deriving from God,
            a universe that has significant powers of its own—
         being an unfolding, progressing manifestation
            of God himself,
            of God herself.
Some of these organisms and circumstances
   resulting in diseases are more readily influenced
      by the healing power of Pure Love,
      and some are less so.
And some diseases, probably all diseases,
   can be more readily influenced and overcome
      by God's will and power through our cooperation
      and collaboration with him, with her
      in this tremendous undertaking.
Actually, it is our supreme purpose,
   as God's crowning achievements and achievers,
      to work in harmonious accord with Pure Love
      to bring about the eradication of every disease.
This is done in a number of ways.

First, throughout the evolution
   of the many species of this world,
      God has answered the inner needs of each species
      to protect themselves from diseases
         by enabling them to develop an interior defense—
         an immunological system.
This has empowered each species currently existing

to survive *as a whole*,
   although individual plants, lower animals, and humans
   still contract or develop diseases sporadically,
   sometimes epidemically.
Being the sensitive, empathetic creatures
   that we human beings are,
      witnessing the majority of our race
      and other species survive
         while a minority suffers and sometimes dies
         holds little consolation.
The afflicted must be helped,
   and it is through this compassion that humankind
   is empowered to help and heal them.

So secondly, the ability to prevent diseases
   and treat those afflicted has been developed
      within humanity through the medical sciences.
For thousands of years, men and women
   have experimented with the substances of the Earth
      to bring about treatments and cures.
Using their imaginations
   and their thirst for healing knowledge,
      physicians throughout history have built upon
      previous successes to arrive at the intricate,
         specialized, and highly advanced arena
         of modern medicine.
And God has been, not only with them,
   but within them every step of the way.

God has also been with, and continues to be with,
   all of those who pray for healing,

who meditate for healing.
Prayer and meditation are the necessary states of mind
  a person must have in order to transfer or receive
    God's cleansing, healing power.
For prayer quiets the mind and engages the will
  in a powerful combination of spiritual activity,
    enabling one to experience and articulate
      their deepest needs—to enter that secret, inner place
    where God is most accessible.
Meditation achieves much the same result,
  focusing the mind through the exclusion
    of outward distractions,
    laying the mental foundation
      for a deeper renewal.
And those masters of these arts
  are much valued persons within the healing arena,
    much akin to physicians and their assistants.

The closer all types of healers become,
  and the more they learn from one other
    and rely on one another,
    the closer we all grow to God, and in God.
For the desire to heal,
  the intuition and imagination needed
    to successfully experiment—the courage to try—
    are qualities near and dear to the very heart and mind
      of our kind and loving God.
That is why healers are so precious to Pure Love,
  who is the Source of all healing.
And the avenues of healing leading out of that Source
  are varied and true.

DISEASE

But the truest of them is the *exalted way*,
   which when embraced
      can inspire the afflicted, empower the healer,
     and disperse the affliction—
        thus healing the body, while purifying the heart,
       and rescuing the mind.

Mental Illness and Disability

The phenomena of mental illness and mental disability,
   although having similarities to other ailments,
      are unique enough to deserve special consideration.
For they are occurrences of the mind—
   the mind being a unique blend of spirit and matter,
      self and brain.
The brain is not the source of selfhood,
   but it is the essential tool
      through which selfhood is expressed
      within the natural universe.
Matter is by no means the source of spirit,
   but it is the necessary medium through which spirit,
      like conscious energy,
      makes its presence known and felt in this world.

For, apart from the possible unmanifested aspects
   of the essence of God,
      only that which is manifested
      can affect and influence life forms, places,
         and things within this universe—
            even if that which is manifested is pure energy.
That's what it means to be a part of the unfolding,

progressing manifestation of God.
Something or someone must be a vehicle
    for that manifestation.
And this is no more apparent than with the phenomenon
    of the animal brain—be it fish, insect, amphibian,
        reptile, bird, lower mammal, or human.
But it is especially apparent with us humans.

For it is the human brain that has developed over eons
    into a more and more complex vehicle
        for the life and expression of each human self.
The human brain is the most effective organ yet discovered
    to act as a sort of gateway to the spiritual realm
        of the individual self.
Each self exists before the development of the brain
    within the human being he or she currently is,
        and each self exists after the death of the brain
        within the human being he or she currently is.

Now, even though an individual self does exist
    before the human brain it is blended with existed,
        and after the human brain it is blended
        with no longer exists,
            it is very possible that the experience
            of the self's spiritual existence
                is somewhat different
                than his or her earthly human existence.
No one can say for sure what it must be like,
    because even those claiming to return
        from a near-death experience
        still had a body and brain to return to.

But it could be similar to our experience
  of existence within the dream realm,
    where flight can occur with a thought,
    and death is but a new awakening.

So it is the human mind—
  coupled with that extraordinarily intricate web of tissue,
    the human nervous system—
    that forms the foundation of existence
      for a human body and being,
      a human person.
And when that mind is damaged
  by infection, chemical imbalances, physical trauma,
    or psychological disturbances,
    the result can be a unique form of disease—
      mental illness.
It is a kind of illness, like any other illness,
    that our loving God does not will,
      that he constantly, persistently strives to eradicate.
With the help and cooperation
  of men and women throughout history,
    in many cases, God has.
As for the continuing existence of mental illness
    in the face of God's will opposing it,
      the explanations previously given also apply here.

God wants every man, woman, and child
    to have a sound, clear, healthy mind.
God desires nothing more for his, for her human offspring.
That is why Pure Love is continually pressing through
    into the natural world to bring about such healing.

But, like when attempting to bring about
   any positive change, any improvement,
      God meets powerful, natural realities—
      realities that can be obstacles to God's will
         because they derive their power
         through their very existence
            from he, from she who is the Purest Love.
That which is manifested in the universe
   has the ability to offer resistance
      to God's power and will,
      even to that power in its fullness—
         but only for a while.

For eventually all natural obstacles
   within this progressing manifestation of God
      will be overcome and transformed
      by the Spirit of God.
It is just a matter of time.
And how long a time really depends on how willing
   the intelligent and self-aware beings
      in the universe are to collaborate and cooperate
      with God's loving power and will.
For with such collaboration, countless obstacles—
   be them physical, chemical, organic,
      psychological, or social—
      can be overcome and transformed into better,
         deeper, more harmonious realities.

And if these obstacles are mental illnesses,
   they can be healed.
If these obstacles are the psychological causes

for mental illness, they can be prevented,
    thus avoided altogether.
For where often physical, chemical, or genetic causes
    of mental illness seem out of our control,
        the psychological causes are sometimes
        very much in our control.
Because it is often what we say or don't say,
    what we do or don't do,
        that can contribute to mental illness in others—
        especially to those in our care.

We must strive to love, respect,
    protect and cherish those in our care,
        even if we haven't been loved, respected,
        protected and cherished enough by those
            who have cared for us.
This can be really difficult to do,
    because it's not always easy to love
        when you feel like damaged goods.
But we have to try anyway, because those in our care
    really need our love and attention in the present,
        not our fear and loathing from the past.
So let's try to let bygones be bygones,
    and rightnows be rightnows.
The cycles of psychological abuse can be broken,
    if the desire is strong enough,
        our love deep enough.

Another harsh reality that deserves deeper consideration
    is mental disability.
Many mental disabilities are the result

of a defect occurring in the womb prior to birth,
   although some do have a physical
   or chemical cause after birth.
Those mental disabilities that are caused before or after birth
   are never willed by our nurturing God,
      never caused to happen by his, by her influence.
Actually, it is God's desire that no human being
   suffer mental disability at any time,
      that every human being be granted a mental capability
      falling in the range of normal.
Whatever the cause of a disability before birth,
   be it certain combinations of blood types in the parents,
      unfortunate diseases during pregnancy,
      metabolic disorders affecting the brain,
         or abnormalities in the genes—
         and whatever the cause of a disability after birth,
            be it oxygen deprivation during delivery,
            illness producing a long, deadly fever,
               or a head injury—
               it is always God's heart-felt will and desire
               that these tragic events,
                  and the disabilities that they produce,
                  never occur, never afflict anyone.

Actually, the same can be said for any defect
   occurring before, during, or after birth.
God did not will it.
God does not want it.
God wants it healed.

But physical defects, mental disabilities, mental illnesses,

and the many causes of all of these things,
are powerful realities in this universe.
They are often made up of countless combinations
of elements, chemicals, compounds, processes,
timing, chance, accidents, and diseases—
all of these being significant realities and occurrences
within this awesome process we are growing
to understand more and more fully
as God's unfolding manifestation,
as God's progressing collaboration with nature.

Yes, God wants all of these afflictions healed,
all of their causes prevented.
How could our all-loving God want anything else?
That is why God so diligently struggles against them,
so eagerly seeks to empower those
who would be healers,
who would join him, join her in combating them.
But overcoming the natural obstacles
to God's work and will is a process,
a process that involves our continuing development
as collaborators with Pure Love and each other—
collaborators for wholeness, happiness,
and healthiness.

This is why God has provided the *exalted way*—
to guide, aid, and nurture us,
to cure our fears and afflictions, to empower us,
and to overcome evil,
once and for all.

Evil

What exactly is evil?
And what are the motivating factors
   behind its occurrences?
Evil is found where a sane, adult person's free
   and deliberate thought, word, and/or action
      unjustifiably harms a being or beings,
      place or places, and/or thing or things.
There are a lot of qualifying words in this definition,
   so let me explain.

In the vast majority of cases, the promoter of evil
   is an individual person or a group of persons—
      currently limited to a human person
      or a group of human persons.
There have been very rare cases
   of lower animals seemingly committing evil,
      like when a lion was known to kill
      for what appeared to be his pleasure alone.
But it can be difficult to determine whether such an animal
   is mentally healthy or even sane,
      and its lower animal nature could very well disqualify
      its actions from being free—

freedom being a quality of high intelligence,
self-evaluation, and a deep understanding
of the consequences of one's thoughts,
words, and deeds.

Also, it is important for the person
to be considered an adult in order for their actions
to be regarded as full-fledged evil.
For if they are not yet an adult, they are still developing
mentally, emotionally, spiritually, and socially—
as well as physically.
This development limits their freedom,
for they do not yet possess the interior free will
to always make the right choices.
They do not understand the wrong that they do,
making it less like evil, and more like ignorance.

In order for an adult person to commit evil,
they must be mentally sane,
for insanity is such a complete disruption
of normal thinking and judgment that, once again,
free will is obstructed,
and often diffused altogether.
The insane can be extremely dangerous,
but their misdeeds cannot be considered
freely calculated evil.

For a thought, word, or action to be evil,
there must be deliberate intent.
A thought can be misguided, an opinion misinformed,
an act an accident, but none of these are evil,

for none are deliberately and intentionally willed.

Also, for evil to be committed,
    some form of harm must be inflicted
        on some person, some place, or something.
If no harm has occurred, then evil is not present,
    for it is the very essence of evil
        to cause pain, inflict suffering—
        to either disable or totally destroy.
The degree to which a sane, adult person's thought,
    word, and/or action harms someone, some place,
        or something determines the degree of evil
        that has been committed.
Many would say that minor harmful thoughts,
    words, or actions should not be considered evil,
        but simply wrongdoing.
But the vast majority of intentional harm done
    should be recognized as some form of evil,
        no matter how slight the hurt,
        no matter how meager the affliction.
From a minor inconsideration to a horrendous crime,
    evil is present, for intentional harm occurs.
It is simply a difference of *degree*.

And the remaining intentional harm inflicted,
    the remaining pain, suffering, disability,
        or destruction caused that is not evil,
            is categorized so because it is justified.
Yes, for evil to be committed,
    the harm inflicted must be unjust.
But to understand what is justified and what is not,

one must have an awareness of what true justice is.
And true justice begins with a spiritual valuing
of persons, lower life forms, places, and things.

Every person, lower life form, place, or thing
in this universe has intrinsic value,
and that intrinsic value derives from God,
from Pure Love.
That value is a quality implicit within this universe—
within any person, any lower being,
any place, or anything that is a part
of this unfolding manifestation of God,
this emerging collaboration of nature with God.

To be a part of God's progressing manifestation
is to have a basic value within the universe—
and in God's eyes.
All members of a given species have this basic value,
just as all places have a basic value, and all things.
The only prerequisite that any of these need
in order to qualify for this basic value
is their existence,
for it is their existence that makes them a part
of the manifestation of God.

And God loves them all.
How could he, how could she who is Pure Love
do otherwise?
God loves all species, places, and things
with a piercing love that reflects the true value
of all species, all places, and all things that exist.

Only God knows just how immense that love is.
But those who have grown close to God
   can become aware of that loving,
      can become attuned to the true value
      of everyone and everything.
This is the very essence of goodness—
   the intrinsic value of everyone and everything
      as derived from God,
      along with the recognition and awareness
         of that value and of God by beings capable
         of such recognition and awareness,
            joined with the love, respect,
            and outward nurturing treatment
               that such an awareness of God,
               and of the true value of everyone
               and everything, promotes.

And the true value of you, of anyone,
   cannot be measured by human standards.
It is that great, that profound.
For instance, your value is not only greater
   than the value of all the diamonds in the world,
      it is greater than the value
      of all the diamonds in the world
         multiplied by a million!

Don't doubt it.
   It's true.

God has collaborated with nature for billions of years
   to bring about your existence.

You are not only a part of this Creation,
    but through your living and breathing,
        your comings and goings,
           you are a participant in God's universe,
               whether you realize it or not.
How you participate during your life
    does not affect your basic value as a participant.
Your existence as a human being
    assures your value as a participant
        within the human family—
        and as long as you are breathing,
           you are participating.
No ignorance you foster, or evil you commit,
    can devalue you as a person in the eyes of God.

What it can do is put you out of God's favor.
And to be out of God's favor
    is an altogether miserable experience.
For to be out of God's favor—to reap God's disapproval—
    is not to be any less valuable a human being
        than anybody else.
To think or say or do something that God disapproves of
    is simply to hurt God,
        and depending on what is done,
        to sometimes hurt God very deeply.
And the reason God is so hurt by the evil that we do
    is because we are harming
        that which God loves and values.
Our loving God is connected to that
    which he, which she loves and values,
        and it is through this connection that God is hurt

whenever we do unjust harm to any person,
  lower being, place, or thing.

When in the midst of these hurtful evil doings,
  if we are honest with ourselves,
    we will discover that God's pain is really our pain—
    that true remorse is God grieving in us,
      with us, and even *for* us.
If we embrace our guilty feelings,
  and let them do their work deep within us,
    we will be drawn into a deeper awareness
    of the true value of everyone and everything.
We will come to understand that the evil we sometimes do
  does not devalue us as human beings,
    but does pierce the very heart of God,
    causing him, causing her to suffer—
      sometimes greatly.
Yes, to grow closer to an authentic understanding
  of true justice is to become aware
    of the intrinsic value of every person,
    lower being, place, and thing.

It's true that humans have more value than lower animals,
  that lower animals have more value than plants,
    that plants have more value than minerals
    and the other elements,
      and that minerals and the other elements
      have more value than space.
But it's also true that the value God places
  on all of these, and the least of these,
    is more complex and profound than we can fathom—

unless we have grown close enough to God
to see through his eyes,
to love through her heart.
Once we have a more authentic understanding
of this genuine value and true justice,
we are better equipped to determine what justifies
a harmful act, and what does not—
what is not evil, and what is.

It appears that a good summation for what justifies
a thought, word, or act that is harmful
is when that harm is inflicted during the protection
of a person, lower being, place, or thing
from the evil perpetrated on them
by another person or persons—
and sometimes even by that very same person—
as a way of protecting them from another,
others, or themselves.
But just what harm should be inflicted, and to what degree,
can be an incredibly delicate matter,
and it doesn't help that it often has to be inflicted
in the heat of the moment, amidst struggle,
sometimes chaos.
However, any degree of struggle or chaos
does not change a justifiable defense into an evil act,
for the intent is not to devalue
the aggressor or aggressors,
but to protect the value and existence
of the victim or victims.

But why does evil occur in the first place?

EVIL

And what factors contribute to its occurrences?

Evil begins where the influence, power, and presence
   of certain manifested phenomena
      overcome the influence, power, and presence
      of God, of Pure Love,
         within a person or persons.
That influence, power, and presence
   of various manifested phenomena
      can occur outside of a person
      as well as within a person.
Another way of saying it is—where the influence, power,
   and presence of God is palpable,
      is strongly felt, keenly experienced,
      the tendency to do evil is greatly diminished,
         and can often disappear altogether.
For the thing that influences a person
   to commit evil is really a desire,
      a desire to alleviate the pain
      of a lack within that person—
         a lack of love, which is hate,
         a lack of tolerance, which is anger,
            a lack of security, which is fear,
            a lack of joy, which is emptiness,
               a lack of communion or community,
               which is loneliness.

Now, the pain of these inner lacks
   can be induced by, or contributed to by,
      the injustices of life that we sometimes suffer—
      especially when a person is still developing

towards adulthood, or is otherwise vulnerable.
If a child is deprived of the basic means of sustaining life,
if he or she is wanting in food, shelter, clothing,
mobility, education, or love —
if a child is violently stripped of any of these things—
then their absence
can most certainly form obstacles
between that developing child and God.
But if the same injustices occur to one who has had
a secure and happy childhood,
who is well grounded in God's love,
that person could very well escape the inner lacks
that plague those less fortunate,
and escape the road so many others take
to alleviate the pain of such lacks.

For a person often reacts out of the desire
to alleviate the pain caused by these lacks
by doing harm to another or to themselves—
by violently taking another's property,
or another's body,
by taking another's life, or their own life.
But it doesn't work because—
granting the aggressor survives—
the pain of a lack is only superficially glossed over,
and festers just under the surface,
to erupt with a deeper fury.
And if the aggressor doesn't survive,
then the precious gift of life itself is lost,
and the very body that felt so much, even that pain,
will cease to feel anything.

No, the only thing that can truly cure
　　such inner deficiencies,
　　　　can actually correct the imbalance of power
　　　　that certain manifested phenomena
　　　　　　have over us and within us,
　　　　　　　is the love and power and presence
　　　　　　　　of our awe-inspiring God.

For God can fulfill our deepest needs—
　　our needs for acceptance, inner joy,
　　　　serenity, understanding, and forgiveness.
And God wants to fulfill these needs, with all his heart.
But the interplay between God
　　and the unfolding universe is such
　　　　that the gentle, ineffable, spiritual activity
　　　　of Pure Love is in contention with this physical,
　　　　　chemical, biological, psychological,
　　　　　and social world—
　　　　　　　particularly the more destructive
　　　　　　　and negative aspects of this world.

For you see, God as the perfect, ageless,
　　all-knowing personal source of nature is Spirit.
Pure Love is by its very essence subtly manifested.
This is why we are not normally bowled over
　　by the activity and influence of God at all times.
It's because the meeting points
　　between God's subtle essence
　　　　and the bodies, hearts, and minds
　　　　of this realm are found in the quiet recesses

of that which is manifested.
But when God's pure, perfect, and fathomless love
   is discovered in such recesses,
      when the obstacles and barriers have fallen away
      and this love overpowers one's heart and mind,
         then we *can* be bowled over by the influence of God,
         and the point of contact radiates
            with a deep and unwavering joy—
            a joy that can tirelessly motivate one
               to perform profound acts of intense caring,
                  thus completing love's activity and purpose.

This inner joy and strength is the direct result
   of God's fathomless love and essence
      overcoming the obstacles inherent
      within manifested reality,
         and permeating one's heart, mind, and body—
         one's whole self.
It is through this kind of experience—
   this communion with God
      and all that he, all that she longs to offer—
      that one comes to discover one's very spirit,
         for one's spirit was born of such communion,
         and is strengthened by further permeation by God.
Our spirits are manifested reflections
   of God's unwavering, ever-living Spirit.
Your spirit is the sanctuary of your mind,
   the altar of your heart,
      where you receive the offerings of God.

And it is these offerings that alleviate the pain

of the lacks that we experience.
It is the joy and strength produced by God's touch
    that can quell the desires for lesser things—
        things that are not rightfully ours,
        things that would unjustifiably harm another
            for us to obtain, to use and possess.
It is the joy of God's touch that is like a healing ointment
    on the open wound of evil's doings and desires.

When someone commits evil,
    it is attributed to that person's faults.
But what contributes to a person's faults?
Are they **F**rightened,
        Angry,
        Undernourished,
        Lonely,
        Tired, or
        Sick?
Before we rush to judge someone as essentially bad,
    let's get to the roots of their sufferings,
        so that we may more fully understand
        why they sometimes commit evil.
It is with such understanding
    that we can approach them as they truly are,
        instead of reproaching them
        for what they sometimes do.

It is through such understanding
    that we can nurture compassion
        toward one who has done wrong,

maybe giving them a glimpse
   of the kind of love God has for them,
     when they might not have discovered it
      on their own.

Evil hurts ...
   it hurts us,
     it hurts the ones we love,
     it hurts the one who commits it,
      it hurts God, who suffers with us all.
But evil will not last forever,
   for as we grow closer to one another,
     as we all grow closer to God,
     evil grows weaker and less destructive
      over the course of time.

And as for Satan,
   I have to say that I've heard much about him,
     but am not aware of having met him,
     so I must rely on the testimony of others.
Many have said,
   and there are those who continue to say,
     that he exists.
The greater danger could lie in doubting them.

But for now, let's move on to the life-altering reality
   of the *exalted way*,
     and its profound effect on humanity.

PART IV

The Interventions

The Chosen

Of all of the known phenomena
  to emerge within the universe,
    none better or more highly reflects
    God's very essence than that of personality,
      lower animal as well as human.
For the essence of God's Self is *personhood*,
  with all of its countless, multifaceted aspects.
And life, deriving from God its reality—
  its ability to change and grow being empowered by God—
    has emerged over billions of years
    from single-celled organisms
      with precious little, if any, personhood,
      to majestic animals and noble humans
        brimming with personhood—
        the light of intelligence and emotion
        shining through their eyes.

Personhood within the natural world
  is expressed more deeply when a living being
    is able to experience the full potential
    of the qualities that they possess
      as an individual member of a species,

primarily the lower animal and human species.
Personhood within God is always expressed deeply
because he, because she is the very *beingness* of life,
who always experiences the full potential
of the qualities that he, that she possesses,
as the one true Source of potential itself,
of qualities themselves.

It is when God's personhood within the spiritual realm
is attempting to press through and be made manifest
in this world that the contention begins,
that the conflict arises.
It is because God's power and presence
is only partially expressed at this time
that evil persons are empowered to live and thrive,
but are not enlightened enough to base their lives
on goodness and truth.
Every good person occasionally harms others
because there is some aspect of their personality
that is blocked off from God's light,
that maybe wasn't allowed to fully develop.
And the greatest aid to God's love
breaking through in a person's life
is the kindness and support of a healthy,
nurturing family.

For God in his, in her all-knowing wisdom
has collaborated with countless species over time
to bring about the wondrous reality of the family—
lower animal, human, and often (through adoption)
a combination of the two.

THE CHOSEN

Once the reality of family was established
    and civilization began,
        God was ever seeking to express his, express her will,
        presence, and power to and through humanity.
This meeting between God and humanity
    manifested itself in many forms, all over the globe.
Primitive religions sprang up and evolved
    as experiences of God deepened.

But these religions,
    with their concepts of gods and more gods,
        fell short of the actual reality
        of just who God was—and *is*.

That is, until the Hebrew people arrived on the scene.
The Jews had a unique desire to know God
    for who he truly was,
        instead of who they wanted him to be.
And Pure Love responded.
God spoke through human mouthpieces,
    enacted miracles through human agencies—
        for a miracle must have a human consciousness,
        a human agency to work through,
            to appear through.
This is why one doesn't see miracles occurring
    among the lower animals,
        because the lower animal consciousness
        is not capable of being a vehicle for such an activity,
            at least at this time.

God's voice rang out through the Hebrew prophets,

with their exhortations and lamentations.
King David was lifted up as a poignant example
   of the servant, turned adulterer,
      then made a better servant again.
God, the author of truth and beauty,
   expressed his oneness, truthfulness, and beauty
      through a people that desired truth
      above their own personal vision of the truth,
         thus receiving it.
And so, the highest example of the people of God
   in ancient times was the Jewish people—
      with their promised land of Israel,
      and their great city, Jerusalem.

And they remained the deepest expression
   of God's people …
      for a time.

The Man

Once his people were well established,
    God sought to provide the ultimate expression
        of himself—
        by becoming a *human being.*
This meant finding the purest vehicle for such a birth,
    for it was only through such a vehicle
        that this ultimate act could take place.
It took centuries,
    but when the ultimate vehicle was found—was born—
        she made it possible by her very presence
        for God to become human.

For she yearned for such a reality,
    yearned with all her heart,
        and like when life itself was born on Earth,
        God met her in her yearning.
God met Mary in her purity and yearning,
    and a child was conceived.

And that child would become the ultimate,
    the *very ultimate manifestation* of Pure Love.
Mary, betrothed to Joseph,

but untouched by him or any other man,
would conceive Jesus.
And a new light would fill the earth.

For Jesus would become the vehicle
through which God's ultimate power
would be made known to humanity.
The very personhood of God was contained in his flesh—
for God and Jesus were *one*.

Jesus came proclaiming
that the Kingdom of God was at hand,
and urged people to reform their lives
and join together in that community.
He told story after story
depicting what that Kingdom was like.
It was like a mustard seed,
a pearl of great price,
a lost coin,
or a lost son, found.

Jesus did wonderful acts, magnificent deeds,
like making the blind to see,
curing the sick, enabling the lame to walk,
offering forgiveness for people's sins,
and raising the dead.
He did these great works,
not only through his connection with God as Spirit,
but also through the faith of those afflicted.
For it is a person's faith that meets God partway
in the miracles of life,

and in Jesus' day
those meetings were more easily made.

I know this from experience.

For as I remember a time of heartache in my life,
and then a conversion of love and joy—
of God's power as I felt compassion
for my children, their mother—
now I know only a hollowness, a numbness,
an emptiness that I never knew existed.
And yet I still have faith in God,
in Jesus' power to heal,
because like the man born blind and made to see,
I have felt his healing love before.

Just not now,
and I don't know why,
for I cry out daily,
but have become burnt-out emotionally
none the less.

But I don't blame God.
I don't blame Jesus.
I believe whatever barriers there are
between God and me,
are within me.

And I still believe in the *exalted way*.

The Exalted Way

After Jesus had ministered for three years,
   after he had instructed his twelve disciples
      in the ways of the perfect community of God,
      he went to Jerusalem—
         for the last time.

There he sat at supper, took bread and gave thanks,
   broke it and gave it to his disciples.
Then Jesus said, "Take and eat—for this is my *body*,
   which is given up for you.
      Do this in remembrance of me."
He then took a cup of wine, gave thanks and said,
   "Drink from this—for this is my *blood*,
      the *blood of the new covenant*,
      which is shed for you."
And with these consecrating words,
   the simple gifts of bread and wine
      were transformed into God's meal, the Eucharist—
      God's meal of oneness and peace.
But it would not end there.

For that night Jesus would go to the garden of Gethsemane.

He would go there and pray—pray for his life,
    pray that there could be some other way than dying
        to bring about salvation for humanity.
But there wasn't.
There absolutely wasn't.

Why not?

Jesus had to die for God's Spirit to fill the Earth
    because Jesus' spirit had to go to God
        for that *connection* to be made
        between Pure Love and the universe—
            establishing a conduit
            between God and humanity.
It was essential that Jesus die,
    because the connection could not be made
        any other way.
Such a conduit between God and this world
    could not be established with a lesser act.

In order to fully understand this,
    one must become aware of a little-known dynamic
        between God and the universe.
When any entity—especially a human entity—
    experiences death,
        they carry back to God within their very spirit
        the essence of their life experience here on Earth.
God draws into himself, into herself each spirit,
    including the essence of that entity's life experience,
        and actually uses that spirit and essence
        to further the processes of evolution—

the processes of physical and spiritual evolution,
as well as the evolution of culture.
This dynamic is called
the breathing in and the breathing out,
and is an essential part of derivism.
It is also the reality that was subconsciously apprehended
by our ancestors when human and animal sacrifices
were offered to God during rituals,
misguided acts based on a kernel of truth—
that God does *breath in* the essence of the departed,
and uses it to *breath out* a renewing power,
an enabling power into the world of the living,
a power for growth and change.

This reality is why Jesus had to die,
not only as a kind of ransom for the sins of all—
an interpretation that was especially useful
for our predecessors,
and is still held dear by many today—
but also as an essential act
in which Jesus' body and spirit
were drawn into God and used,
used by God who is Pure Love
to establish a sacred conduit
for the activity of the Holy Spirit.

For once Jesus Christ died, was buried,
and was resurrected—
was *breathed in and breathed out*
by God our Source—
it truly became possible for the Holy Spirit,

. which is God's working activity on Earth,
to play upon this universe in an amazing
and unprecedented way—
a way that began at Pentecost,
is still happening today,
and always will happen.

To believe this is to embark on the *exalted way*.

The *exalted way* is this—
to know that God is Pure Love,
to experience this reality during one's life,
to recognize that this experience
comes through the acts of Jesus' living
and dying and rising,
that God used Jesus' body and spirit—
Christ's very essence
as the embodiment of God—
to form a conduit between Pure Love
and the universe,
a living conduit for all
who would receive the Holy Spirit,
who *could* receive the Holy Spirit.

For the reception of the healing Spirit of God
is not a certain thing,
even if one believes in the reality of Jesus Christ.
One has to be open to it, in many ways.
My experience has been that the more compassionate,
merciful, and loving a person is prone to being,
the more likely it is that the Holy Spirit

will burst in on them.
They must be ready to receive it—
    psychologically, physiologically,
        as well as chemically.
It's not enough to just believe, one has to be conditioned,
    and that conditioning must be done
        with thoughtfulness and care.
This is true for everyone.

But when a person has been made readied,
    and the inner obstacles have fallen away,
        then the healing power coursing through that person—
        the power of the living Christ, of our loving God—
            can accomplish amazing things.
For this is how miraculous events actually come about,
    through the hearts, minds, spirits, and limbs
        of each person who has been made an actual vehicle
        within which the power of Pure Love moves.

The results might not be immediate,
    or appear to be what we expect them to be,
        but if we hold on to the truth
        that God really does only want the best
            for us and those we love,
            then we will see in our daily lives his workings,
                and be drawn into living an *inspired life*.

That is, if we can keep the effects
    of the harsher realities
        of everyday life at bay.

An Inspired Life

Once devotion to Jesus has been cultivated,
   once real and true contact
      with God the Source has been made,
      one must embark on a new way of life,
         to remain true to the relationship
         that has been established
            between oneself and God—through Jesus.
This is not easy, often far from it,
   for many of the ways of modern society
      are not the ways of God, of Jesus.
And sometimes this newly found life of Jesus
   emerges within a person when they are entangled
      in a web of worldly relationships,
      modern-day institutions,
         and demanding work.

If a person doesn't have adequate support from life—
   like a nurturing church, supportive family,
      or fulfilling occupation—
      then the realities of everyday existence can consume
         this new fragile life of God
         that is emerging within a person,

this fresh joy that wants to gain a foothold
in a person's life.

Believe me, I speak from experience.

I did have a supportive family,
   and I did have a nurturing church,
      but my occupation,
         which I needed to support my wife and children,
            was not fulfilling, did not nurture
            this new and fragile life of Christ
               that had erupted into my life.
And my marriage,
   which at times was a source of nurturance,
      also caused me much desperation.

So I know what it is to lose.
I know what it is to feel the glory and power
   of Jesus for a time,
      and then to lose all feeling in the midst of crisis,
      of trauma that is unrelenting—
         the past, present, and future trauma
         that plays on a sensitive mind and soul,
            until that soul is broken.

But I remember …
   I remember the joy of holding newborns,
      the breathing of a strong lover,
      the soul-shattering experience of conversion,
         when I realized that I would never be the father
         I had always wanted to be,

and that my children would be hurt by that.

Then I was flooded,
    flooded with love and joy,
        a love and joy that was with me
        for over ten years,
            before it was swallowed up
            in the cares of the world.

But I remember,
    so I write from memory.

An *inspired life* is this—
    to live and work in a God-filled community,
        to share what you have with your neighbors,
        to seek peace, to work for social justice,
            to love God with your whole self,
            to spread the news about Jesus, in word and deed,
                to not blame God, not blame Jesus
                when tragedy occurs,
                    because you understand that God is offering
                    everything in his, in her power, through Jesus,
                    but that this offering
                        is in constant contention,
                        in constant struggle
                        with the natural universe,
                            a universe that derives from Pure Love,
                            is an unfolding manifestation of God.

This belief system is Christian derivism,
    and it can be a steadfast friend

to anyone embarking on the *exalted way.*

This *exalted way* is a path
   that I may *never* be able to walk again,
      as I cry out from these emotional depths.

It is a way that I can only point to,
   from the memory of where I once stood before …

A Matter of Balance

Hell is real.
At least hell on Earth is real.
  This I know.
The severe depression that hijacked my brain chemistry
    and laid siege to my mind
        caused me to plummet into a numbness and isolation
        that can only be equated to a living hell.
But there is a way back from hell,
    a way back to the land of hope,
        peace, and joy.

It takes time, treatment, and tenacity—
    the *three T's of recovery.*

Few cures are instantaneous,
    and even if they appear to be so
        there are still lingering effects that take time
        to be healed in their entirety.
It's important to accept that wholeness
    isn't experienced overnight.
But what can happen overnight is a *turning point*—
    a hitting bottom, a saving hand up.

Always remember,
    no matter how desperate things get,
        no matter how dire the situation,
        life can turn on a dime.
Never underestimate that possibility,
    and never doubt it.

It's just a matter of seeking treatment—
    the second *T of recovery*—
    and trusting that it will be found.
That treatment can be talk therapy, medication,
    group support, art therapy, exercise,
        nutrition, prayer, meditation—
        or any combination of these things.
The important thing is to find the right treatment,
    to trust that it will make things better,
        and to know that God is the healing source
        behind any truly effective therapy.

I know this from personal experience.

I've felt the anguish of severe depression,
    of tumbling into a full-fledged emotional breakdown,
        of lying in bed at night in a tortured state,
        with nothing but a Bible clutched to my chest
        to serve as an anchor for my sanity.
And then to awaken the next morning to a *turning point*,
    knowing that somewhere in the night,
        life had turned on a dime.

A MATTER OF BALANCE

That morning was a new start,
 a slow climb upwards,
  but a climb that brought renewed feelings
  of hope, peace, and joy.
It was also a climb that required me
 to leave aspects of my old life behind.

I survived that breakdown, that depressive episode,
 but my marriage did not.
My relationship with my children flourished
 during that time of healing,
  but my relationship with their mother deteriorated,
  and ended in divorce.
Some things should come to an end,
 in order for better things to follow.

Now, years later, I am remarried to a wonderful woman,
 and I am thriving in a way I have never thrived before.
I have looked for signs of God's approval of this,
 and have found them written on my very heart.
I thank God that I had the tenacity to seek out wholeness,
 and to pursue my heart's desire.

For tenacity truly is the third requirement—
 the third *T of recovery*—
  which helps one to recover
  from any ailment or circumstance.

We must never, never, *never* give up.
In the midst of despair,
 hold on to that glimmer of hope,

and you will discover God, who is Pure Love,
holding on to you.

The reality of the *three T's of recovery*
can also be applied to the ills of society as well.
But when addressing these ills,
a special significance should be placed on the *balance*
between time, treatment, and tenacity.

We should all want to promote the causes
that God holds dear,
that he, that she wants to bring about in the universe,
as it progresses towards a more and more
authentic manifestation of God.
Many of these causes can be summed up in four words—
put living beings first.
And the higher the life form a living being is,
the more of a priority he or she is given.

We should especially strive with God
to eliminate all human suffering,
whether that suffering is from hunger, war, disease,
natural disasters, accidents, disabilities, addictions,
evil, isolation, and the withholding of civil rights—
as well as all forms of abuse.
The elimination of these things
is God's cherished endeavor,
and it should be ours as well.
But the will and desire to eradicate them
cannot be forced on a person,
or on a society as a whole.

A MATTER OF BALANCE

And that's where the *balance* comes in.

True sustained progress for the good of all in this world
    is brought about through an organic balance
        between an effective treatment of a societal ill,
        the time it takes for the members of a society
          to recognize and address that ill,
          and the measure of tenacity those members use
            in bringing about a solution to that ill.
This matter of balance in bringing about positive change
    can be observed throughout human history,
        and can be witnessed today.
It can especially be viewed in the realm of politics,
    because, let's face it,
        it's within the realm of politics
        that so many of the ills of society are addressed.

The political process should be a balanced endeavor
    between those who want freedoms, the means to live,
        and justice for everyone—as soon as possible—
        and those who oppose that the sharing
          of these things by the ones who hold them
          in abundance be made mandatory—
            usually made so by taxes, regulations, or laws.
The political process should be a balanced undertaking
    between those who want a redistribution of wealth
        by the government through programs,
        and those who feel the acquisition of the means to live
          should be made primarily through private enterprise,
          personal ambition, competition, and self-reliance.
It is a process that should be a balanced effort

between those who want to grant welfare to people in need
through government entitlements,
and those who feel that such assistance
should be more a matter of personal responsibility—
often in the form of private charities.

The endeavor for balanced progress—
one that is of special interest to God—
should be a cooperative effort
between political groups,
between political parties.
But in many cases it turns into an all-out political war.

Groups form into factions, ideologies become solidified,
and very little gets done in the way of actual progress.
For cooperation with each other,
like collaboration with God,
is the way that progress moves forward in peace.
The roles of *us* and *them*
have to be organically broken down
to become simply *we*—
we the people,
we the living beings of Earth,
and hopefully someday, beyond our Earth.

One way of accomplishing this is to withdraw
from the political process long enough
to view the political spectrum from the outside.
Doing this can help one see
that those embracing radical ideologies,
persons or groups on the left as well as the right,

are trying to enact their agendas—
  whether through change
  or the resistance to change—
    in ways that are harmful to people,
    lower life forms, places, or things.
The best way to bring about life-affirming progress
  is found closest to the center of the political spectrum—
    a moderate, cooperative, collaborative approach
    to lasting, effective change.

And the key to all positive, enduring change is *balance.*

There also must be a balance in life
  between the spiritual and the material.
Just as the spiritual cannot be neglected,
  the material aspects of our lives
    cannot be neglected either.
This was a common mistake made
  by some of our ancestors
    when they attempted to purge themselves
    of their desires for material things,
      even their sexual desires for another's body—
      all in the name of God,
        and God's Kingdom.

But it didn't work back then,
  and it doesn't work to this day.

We are a combination of spirit and matter.
And we can never sacrifice one to the other,
  and remain on the road to happiness.

We are made to enjoy material things
as well as spiritual realities.
But enjoying them doesn't mean hoarding them,
so we must cultivate a desire to share what we have—
materially as well as spiritually—
with those less fortunate than ourselves,
and also with those as fortunate
or even more fortunate than we are.

It is this giving attitude of heart and mind,
an attitude after God's own Heart and Mind,
that best furthers the presence of God in the world,
that best brings about the manifestation
of Pure Love, of Divine Wisdom,
into the universe.
It is through my attempt to embrace
this kind of giving attitude
that I have eagerly and openly shared
this philosophy of derivism with you,
and have elaborated on the *exalted way*—
that I have knocked on God's door,
sent out my questions and yearnings,
and reported back to you these impressions,
like echoes from the depths of time.

But these soundings are not the whole story.

They can't be, for I am only one person,
and there are over seven billion of us—
all with our own questions and yearnings sent,
all with our own impressions to receive.

So go for it!

Open your heart and mind a little more each day,
    listen to what God is whispering in your ear,
        and gaze upon what he, what she has to reveal to you.

And when you receive your own answers,
    like any receiver being tuned to an allusive frequency,
        pray that your heart and mind are pure
        in receiving them.
For when it comes to apprehending spiritual matters,
    two things ring true …

One's soundings,
    anyone's soundings,
        are only as sound as the heart and mind
        of the one sending them out—
        of the sounder.

And the soundest hearts and minds
    are the ones bathed in love.

10437909R00087

Made in the USA
Charleston, SC
04 December 2011